Season 4
Redemptive Spirits

Written by Kevin Horton

Illustrated by Daryl Horton

Abolitic · South Carolina

Publisher: Abolitic
For information contact the author at: www.abolitic.com
Cover, Art, and Design by Daryl Horton
Printed in the United States of America.

First Edition: August 2024
Library of Congress Control Number: 2024915751
PRINT: ISBN: 978-1-945047-22-0

This book is dedicated to my sister, Nefertiti Horton. Rest in peace, sis. I also want to dedicate this book to all those who face the struggles of life with its ups and downs. Just know that all of your ups and downs come together to confirm that you have a heartbeat, and life can only reassure you that you shall continue to live. Keep on living... "They that wait on the Lord shall renew their strength; they shall mount up on wings as eagles! They shall run and not be weary, they shall walk and not faint!" Let's go!

And the Lord said, If ye had faith as a grain of mustard seed, ye might say unto this sycamine tree, Be thou plucked up by the root, and be thou planted in the sea; and it should obey you.

- Luke 17:6

Preface

In the quiet corners of our hearts, where shadows dance and doubts linger, there exists a flicker of light that can guide us through the darkest of times. It is faith and belief that ignite this flame, offering solace and strength when uncertainty veils our path. It is in these moments, when our spirits waver, that we find the power to hold on, to persevere, and to emerge stronger than before.

This collection of poetry is a testament to the potency of faith and belief in the face of adversity. Through verses woven with raw emotion and tender vulnerability, we embark on a journey that explores the depths of the human experience. We delve into the intricate tapestry of faith—whether it be rooted in religion or spirituality—and discover the transformative power it holds. Within these pages, you will encounter poems that resonate with the ache of despair, the weight of sorrow, and the burden of doubt. Yet, intertwined with these shadows are glimmers of hope, rays of light that pierce through the darkness. Through the lens of faith, healing becomes possible, and redemption takes shape.

This collection invites you to reflect on the unwavering strength that emanates from embracing your beliefs. These poems are a reminder that faith is not merely an abstract concept, but a guiding force that can anchor us during life's tempestuous storms. It is an invitation to seek solace and guidance when the world feels fragile, to find meaning in the midst of chaos, and to cultivate a deeper connection with the divine.

I delve into the process of transformation and renewal. Here, you will encounter poems that bear witness to the healing power of vulnerability, forgiveness, and resilience. Like a phoenix rising from the ashes, these verses illuminate the journey towards redemption, reminding us that pain is not the end, but a catalyst for growth and renewal.

As you embark on this poetic odyssey, I invite you to open your heart and mind to the possibilities that lie within. May these verses serve as a guiding light, igniting the flames of faith and belief within you. May they inspire you to hold steadfast in the face of adversity, to embrace the healing that comes from within, and to find redemption and power on the other side of pain.

For it is in the exploration of faith and belief, and in the pursuit of healing and redemption, that we uncover the true essence of our humanity—a tapestry of resilience, hope, and unwavering strength.

The Cycle

Savannah MBTC

It is such a blessing to come to a place

where God's presence is here,

It's pleasantly graced

with an atmosphere

that says, "at last I am here."

Where I can seek God's face,

Let go of my past and cast away my fears,

Remove all doubt and embrace my tears.

God has called me out to run this race,

But this time I'm running where God's set the pace,

Whatever it takes I'm committed to win,

At the start with my heart, I said I was all in,

In my desperation a decision between life and death I

was facing, I said I was all in,

In my last fall I said I was all in,

When someone from here answered my call, I said I was all...IN!

See..I took a dive and Christ kept me alive and deep down inside

when I thought that there was nothing left in me,

God once again blew his breath in me!

And gave me an expectancy!

What His excellency expects in me,

And in this season at SMBTC, a new hope and desire to fulfill my destiny has resurrected in me!

Thank you, Jesus, for the revelation that you never give up, you never give up

On replacing misplacements.

And this is the very reason we give Him thanks and praise Him! Kingdom!

Overcoming

Times are changing

as well as emotions

rocking my ship

with the sails wide open,

I'm watching the bow

vigilantly hoping

that my substance increases

by the evidence I'm holding

and as I look around

in this ocean of emotions

I feel so alone at times

when I hear so much commotion

so I go deeper focusing

on the words from those chosen

to lead me through

to keep me going.

At the time my anchor drops

I'm told to be still

and my anger stops

then I know He's real

and I fainted not

His promise is sealed

indeed and locked

reminding me when I forgot,

I have faith to believe

I'll reach the top

and reach the peak

to release nonstop

the Christ in me

for the nation to see

that though this ship

may never sail no more

I'll begin to swim,

I'll get on board,

I'll grab a peace

and with Christ in me

I'll reach the shore

in the end

we win our Father's stepped in

and He's now keeping score.

Battles at Night

Father,

in the day I pray for peace

I plan and I seek

for your Spirit to release

and create in me

a place to be

at night when I sleep

and I dream and see

battles and wars developing in me

spiritually, my expectancy

is expecting to see me

overcoming enemies victoriously

and even in the dark

when my faith is low

I pray in the dark

your light will glow

increase my hope

and then I will know

and then I will know

that with confidence I'll go

and that the battle is won

and it's already done

it's already done

in Jesus Name

Amen!

Love Lost

Have you seen love?

I'm desperately trying to find it,

left my side at a time when I was blinded,

every relationship I encountered I'm reminded

of how sensual and how sweet,

how much peace love gave me to sleep

thoughts of love I imagine

forever lasting

always happening

my emotions are seeking

my heart is asking

for this lost treasure

my spirit is mapping

my soul has measured

the time I'm trapped in

follow the signs

and then I will find.

This one of a kind gift

that He's gifted me

a type of lift

that has uplifted me

a wind that's drifted me

to sail

in a sea destined to prevail

a message from God's mail

in the form of a letter

that binds our souls together

unites us the hold forever

I know that forever

we can make it through any type of weather

love has infiltrated and integrated

our needs and desires

puts out smoke only to stir up fires

inside, the flames get higher

we rise the same our lives are wired

and the connection has came

He told me to write it down and make it plain

I'll read it aloud and I will proclaim

what once was lost shall be found again

In Jesus Name

In Jesus Name!

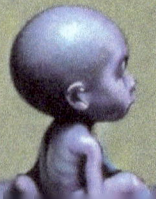

Thoughts or No Thoughts

I don't know if

all my thoughts

are

all my thoughts

or

thoughts that my thoughts brought with them,

because,

some of my thoughts could get lost in thought

and,

I certainly don't think that I would miss them!

Self-Sabotage

Self-sabotage

is a form of self-camouflage

Hiding yourself

from success's entourage

Success comes by to see

that you are so much more

And you digress,

only to tell success

that you are so much less.

And you continue to hide

and believe all your lies,

and you continue to hide

in all your mess.

I must proclaim

and I must profess,

That I am coming

out of this mess,

I am staking my claim,

God knows my name,

I am not the same

This to shall past

this storm will not last

in Jesus Name!

In Jesus Name!

Amen!

TJLG!

Now I Know

When the wind goes by

the atmosphere shifts

right pass my eye

as if, I didn't catch the drift

as if, it was in disguise as a gift

maybe I would've missed it only if,

if it was trying to hide

like I try to hide

the light inside

beside the cry inside

behind the why inside

yet still I rise

to so many ears

and so many eyes.

Now I know.

Knowing You is Like

Knowing you is like riding on the back of an eagle's

wings

while the eagle soars the caged bird sings

because of the protection the protector brings

leave you wanting for more and ready for change

right down to my core nothings the same

you've struck my heart with perfect aim

love right from the start from the moment you came

Knowing you is like walking in a valley on mountain tops

springing with water that never stops

constantly lifting me higher and never drops

fulfilling my desires deep in my bones

I feel your fire I'm never alone

our love is admired and very well known

I'm now stronger and wiser all because of my
cornerstone

Knowing you is like
never having to fear another day in my life
you are always here to make things right
you guide my soul you're my guiding light
that's why I walk by faith and not by sight
that's why I love it when we leap and take flight
and I'm riding on the back of my eagle's wings
and when we soar I love to sing
what knowing you is like!

Behind The Door

Time has passed and in my mind

there's a door I find

that has never been open

and I've increased my hoping

that soon I will see

soon I will be able to be

and be able to have the key

to this door that I walk close and near to

so connected I wish I could peer through

another part of me will appear to be,

another start for me where love sparked in me

the final part and piece of me

to make me complete so completely I can see

my love is in God and God's Love is in me!

Open Book

My desires are changing

the more I am living, loving, and learning,

the fire is still raging

and inside of me

is still yearning

every page is exciting

as I become more aware

that my father is writing

the more I began believing

that life is way bigger

than what I'm seeing

the more fruit I'm eating

every time there's a new season

I'm continually seeking

for a definitive reason

for me living what they're reading

me giving and they're receiving.

John 8 36

We are all invited,

and the only thing required is that you believe.

I believe so much I wear my heart on my sleeve,

I've seen so much I know Christ is all I need,

I release so much because of all His light I've received,

I grieve so much remembering all the times I bleed,

I read so much because these are the times I feed,

so, I can be full and complete,

so, I can be vigilant and take heed,

so that anything he's doing in my life now is done

indeed.

He wrote it!

His Love Lives

My social skills have put in their resignation

around the time I begin spiritually embracing

my destiny and my placement

at the same time I was misplacing

the good choices I was supposed to be making

misguided paths I begin taking,

taking years of time in unfamiliar places

seeing unfamiliar faces

doing things unfamiliar and wishing I could erase this

along with all the chases

but God! My God said

that I am more than able to face it

he's given me great gifts

and how sweet His amazing grace is,

taking me to higher places

the reflection of a facelift

a connection and a closer relationship
what it feels like when God is embracing
one of His to a loving place to live!
Amen!

Discernment

Every moment taken in

are moments I pray within

for God to give me

the ability to stay with Him

after the decisions I make with Him

there are things that I say within

to understand if the next step I take

is real or is fake

so the next choice I make

in Spirit to relate to my soul

when I hear it and He takes control

so when I see Grace I'm bold

and I obtain

to live is Christ

and to die is gain,

I walk by faith

and not by pain

I've corrected my mistakes

by letting go of the shame

I wake up everyday

by calling His name

the atmosphere shift

and my life is changed

as long as I keep

His will in range

I take a step back and I analyze

every moment I see through spiritual eyes

so I can easily see the sin in disguise

so my flesh is subdued and my Spirit will rise.

I resist the devil and my God is glorified.

Selah.

Affected By Learning

Daily I'm paying attention

to every second that's pre-written,

I ponder the questions

and I gasp at indentions,

I'm relentlessly living

to find out what's God's intentions.

There's times when I feel

His quotation marks

My spirit sparks,

He lights my heart.

Ignited I start to take flight,

Only to find that my load is too heavy,

So, I read more hoping one day I'll be ready,

And as I continue to breathe more steady,

I can see where I am heading

and I know it's the beginning,

And though it's a new chapter

I know I'm still wining.

In Him I stay leaning,

So, I can be an affective canvas,

reflection of what I am reading,

My life has new meaning,

The fire in me keeps burning,

Exclamation points at every turn and,

I continue to grow and read and believe,

That I'm effective cause

I've been affected by learning!

Trusting Again

I'm not sure

I know trust anymore,

the last time I saw him

he was mad at me

for believing and being deceived

and he has since been grieving

and in need of worthy

to see him again maybe

they can mend their differences

become trustworthy

and then block out any interferences

bring healing to any hurting

faith is behind the scenes working

my Spirit is constantly praying

and hope continues hoping in the day when

I'll trust again is when

I learn to put away all my doubts

and put all my trust in Him Amen!

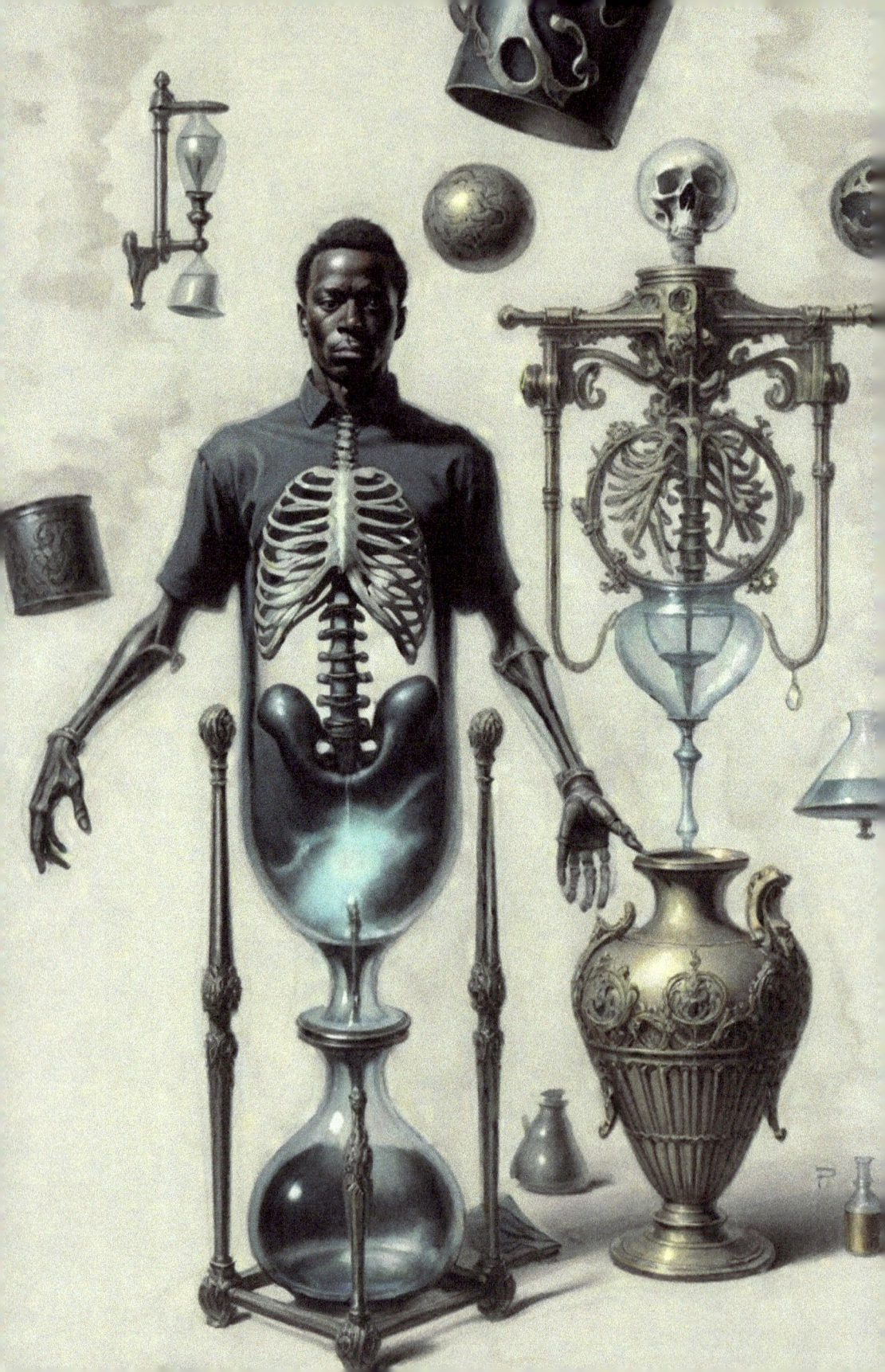

While I'm Waiting

What I know and believe

has changed so drastically

my reality is now fashioning me.

It's like a fantasy

where fiction and fact is impacting me,

it's breaking me and also healing me

it pours out of me

only to come back and begin filling me

creating a feeling in me

in a place that the indwelling is

there it's so compelling

the power of travailing

changing the atmosphere

at last after the fear

has past

we lay down in green pastures

loving on our God and Master

loving harder and faster

love lifted and caught up and raptured

His love in me has been captured

now I see the caption

the living Word in action

the passion

of breathing and believing is happening

releasing and receiving,

praying, and interceding,

patiently awaiting for the day

we all come to the meeting.

You Had Me at Hello

Releasing my feelings

is like listening to my pain

at the same time feeling my healing

from a distance it's insane

to love this feeling

and to think that his feeling

could erase my pain,

take me to a place

where love calls my name

where love is embraced

in a place where love is always the same,

there's no hallways of shame

you are fulfilled at any moment

like the first time you came

a rhythm in your thoughts

that continues to sing

to your heart in sync

with your heart beat

the part where

the spirit of two hearts meet

agape is released

joy and peace seeks

the beat beats

constantly on repeat

Self-Control

Self-Control is the Spirit of a Sound Mind,

a command presence that's always felt the authority that

surrounds time,

a blessing of great divine.

To have life and control it,

making decisions with confidence and boldness,

not knowing what the future holds,

but having an assurance of who holds it.

The mind set to have your mind made up and prepared

for whatever weather you may face,

and to face whatever you go through knowing you go

through it with God's grace.

The knowledge to place,

God before every decision and situation,

so that nothing opposite of His grace,

can come in and steal, kill, or even think of penetrating

the final state or destination.

Self-Control is a Spirit that God gives freely,

to all those needingly

will acquire it exceedingly,

and seizing

the moment in the season

to see the reason

it was given.

To have a sound mind is the beginning of Godly living.

Out On A Limb

To be out on a limb is to commit totally and completely

even when your best is not competing

and the slightest wind could send you fleeing

stuck out here with nothing but other limbs leafing

but still believing

that even though we are on a limb we are still intrigued

at how we are still connected to the tree

and that means we can still see seeds

and that means we can still have our being

no matter what storm or season

being on this limb still gives us a reason

to believe in reasoning,

see, we are constantly out here

in the atmosphere where

the atlas is not clear

surrounded by the aspects of doubt, low self-esteem and

fear,

depression and addiction,

gifts inside of us,

that were once relevant

have become missing,

temptation relentlessly pressing,

intentions are intentionally second guessing,

constantly being tested

and wondering how am I now being tested

when I haven't even digested

the lessons for this testing...

Testing testing one two

testing testing one two three four

testing constantly to see

if the Word that's inside of me can speak clearly

in the mic of my life

so that being out on this limb can increase

how I receive and release

the light in my life

and the communication line is still open

so if what I am hearing is right in my life

then the limbs are where the fruits

are where the tree send all the nutrients in the juice

from the roots are where leaves speak nothing but the

truth

are your experiences on this limb are there to boost

and make you stronger so that new growth will break

loose

and your daily supply of energy will last that much

longer

you begin releasing oxygen to breath

and yes you are still connected to the tree

and being on this limb just has increased

your ability to believe

that as long as you are connected to the true vine

you are connected to true signs

you are truly divine

the righteous one of a kind

of piece to this perfect picture of immaculate design,

One body,

One soul,

One Spirit,

One Tree,

One True Vine,

One mind!

Kingdom!

After the Bite

The man,

who found a beaten and broken snake on the side of the

road,

who took the snake home fed it nurtured it and tended

to it's wounds.

Once the snake had recovered enough,

The snake bit the man.

This is the conversation, after the bite.

The man:

I came along this path and found you in pain, I took you

in, fed you, I had nothing to gain, I let you stay with me

all this time, I was sent to help you, it was clearly a sign,

were you just pretending to like me? I don't understand

snake, why did you bite me?

The snake:
You knew who I was and what I was when you took me in. I was born a snake and a snake I've always been.

I can't change the way I look I'm low to the ground so I have to stay down low so I'll always be low down, I swallow everything whole now, my appetite does not allow me to share, you came down to me and it would seem as though you cared, that's something I couldn't believe cause down this low everyone is deceiving but since you believed in me I allowed you to continue believing.

The Man:
Yes I believed in you, Everyone deserves a chance to heal, even snakes, I've walked down your path so I know

what it takes, I saw your hurt and I too can relate, there was a time I was in pain and someone saved me and helped me along the way, I thank God for His mercy and the kindness of His Grace.

The snake:

But that's not the state I'm in, I bit you because I hang with snakes for the longest this is the place I've been, while you we're tediously tending to my needs, my thoughts were constantly scheming, as much as I tried to change my mind my emotions kept misleading, my heart is always grieving, coping with desires from my flesh I begin seeking whom I may devour and eating, although you're words brought peace in me when you began speaking, for a moment it felt relieving so I would ask that you forgive me but right now what I'm seeing is that my poison is starting to sink in and your life is slowly seeping and soon you will be peacefully sleeping.

The Man:

You poor snake you think you're the first snake I've saved, see I've saved many snakes and many of them still misbehave, and I've survived many bites although many others get their lives right, they stop going down this wrong path and begin traveling in the light, see my strength is in my faith and not in my sight, I see you not as a snake that's low down, I see you as a soul needing to be whole now, a soul longing for God to mold now, you are one step from coming out as pure gold now, confess and stand bold snake this is your new life you've passed away the old, you can now let go of the lies you were told, snake I bind the spirit of fear and loose power, love, and a sound mind which is self control, snake are your ready to go, your skin is beginning to shed, I'm seeing your growth the old you is dead, it's time you forget what's behind and begin looking at what's ahead, I forgive you, this is what the Spirit tells me cause this is what God has said.

Snake:

You are right Sir I'm feeling my skin is shedding, it's time I go for what's right and that's right where I'm heading, I'm thankful for you forgiving, I will no longer live life low down and I will seek for higher living, farewell Sir you've been better to me than all of my snake friends, and I shall visit them so that I can make amends, and maybe even show them the right way maybe even start a new trend, now that I have a new skin a new life I shall begin.

The end!

About the Author

Kevin Horton, a native of Columbia, South Carolina, and a graduate of Eau Claire High School, is a poet, author, minister, U.S. Army veteran, and college student. He holds an Associate's degree in Business Administration and is soon to enroll in his Master's Program in Psychology with a concentration on PTSD and Substance Abuse. Kevin is also a proud father of two beautiful daughters.

Kevin's work centers around faith, belief, healing, and redemption. Through the captivating art of creative writing, he delves into the struggles of humanity, exploring them through the lens of spirituality. With heartfelt intention, Kevin aspires to provide meaningful support to those in need, guiding them to comprehend how to fight like Job and walk like Paul.

Join him on a transformative journey where the power of words intertwines with the resilience of the human spirit.

Upcoming Titles

Soon to come:

Season 3 : Kept in the Lost and Found Place...........

www.ingramcontent.com/pod-product-compliance
Lightning Source LLC
Chambersburg PA
CBHW062017040426
42447CB00010B/2029